T0195566

BUILD YOUR FINANCIAL HOUSE

MATTHEW A. SMITH

authorHOUSE®

AuthorHouse™
1663 Liberty Drive
Bloomington, IN 47403
www.authorhouse.com
Phone: 1 (800) 839-8640

Published by AuthorHouse 04/10/2019

ISBN: 978-1-7283-0724-4 (sc)
ISBN: 978-1-7283-0723-7 (hc)
ISBN: 978-1-7283-0722-0 (e)

Library of Congress Control Number: 2019903963

CONTENTS

CHAPTER 1

WHY?

As I started to write this book I went back and forth on how to start. I thought about just jumping right in to how to do build your financial house and win with money. Yet, I kept coming back to one question. Why? Why am I writing this book? Why should people read it? Finally, why would people want to learn how to build their financial house and what is their motivation?

I'll start with my first why. Why am I writing this book? I wanted to write this book to help people learn to win with money. When I went to look for books on money and how to win with money I found that many of them jumped right into investing. How to invest your money, what were the best investments, even how to time the market! That is all good and well but there is a bigger problem in our country right now. Some studies say that up to ¾ of households live paycheck to paycheck and can't handle a $1000 emergency. People are drowning in student loan debt and car payments they can't afford and over 57 million Americans have no emergency fund. One emergency could turn their lives upside down and they may have to turn to drastic measures to make ends meet. Again, I think investing is very important and you should do it as soon as you can, but you have to have your finances in order and simply have to have money first to invest. There's no reason to have money in the stock market if you can barely buy food or have tons of debt. You won't win with money that way. I wanted to write a book that starts from the beginning. I wanted to write a book for those who want to change their lives starting now. I want you to have the feeling of freedom that I now have when you build your financial house correctly. We don't have a million dollars in investments at this point. Hopefully one day we will and towards the end of the book I will give you the basics of beginning investing and tell you what we do, but I'm not here to tell you how to make a million dollars in a few years (and if someone tells you they can teach you how, run away fast). I'm here to help you get started so you can eliminate debt and have extra money to then start investing and building wealth and simply enjoy your life without having to worry about every little expense. I'm here to help you take the first steps in financial freedom and tell you how my wife and I did it and are continuing to do it.

Throughout this book I will tell you stories about people I have met, where I came from financially and where we were. Most importantly I will tell you where we are now and where we are on our way to. I see and hear about so many people struggling financially like we were and worse. I see so many people that one little hiccup in their financial lives throws them in a tailspin or one time of not getting paid as much as they thought turns into a financial crisis. It hurts me to see people having problems financially when I know that with a little work, things can be much better for them. I want to help you get out of the financial rut and eventually live life like you have always wanted to, but never really thought you would.

So why should you read this book? In this book I will set out the steps to building a strong financial house. I will hopefully make you think about things a little differently and guide you on a journey to having a happy financial life. I will tell you first hand that if your financial house is not in order, the rest of your life won't truly be in order either. Money issues are the biggest reason for fights in relationships and you and your partner must be on the same page with money. If only one of you are working towards a goal, it will either never happen or take twice as long with many arguments in between (and lots of resentment on both sides). Even if you don't have a lot of money or can't afford what you really want right now, the small wins along the way and the "light at the end of the tunnel" will keep you motivated and will let you know that things will be ok and everything will be better soon.

So, why would people want to learn how to build their financial house? I will tell you that the difference for me and how I feel about our life is totally different now from a few years ago. Back then, paying bills was a chore and trying to figure out how we would ever pay off our debt drove me crazy. The thought of buying something fun or the thought of going on vacation only stressed me out more. Now, after building our financial house correctly, it's like a ton of bricks has been lifted off my shoulders. Now paying bills is…well almost fun. The bills get paid with no problem. It's no longer, how are we going to pay all the bills, its how MUCH can we put towards one, or what do we want to do with the extra money.

While we are still on a budget (and always will be) as we are paying the last few bills off, things are so much easier and we are looking towards the future and what we want to do more now. The budget no longer tells us what we can't do, it tells us how much we CAN do. I LOVE trips and vacations and staying in hotels. This used to not happen much and when it did we looked for the cheapest, but safe for us and the kids, hotel and all I thought about was where is the money coming from to pay for this, and every time we found something else we wanted to do, it stressed me out how much it was going to cost and at times ruined the experience for me and my family because of my grumbling about the cost. Now, we budget for vacations and can pick what hotels we want to stay in, not just look for the cheapest. When emergencies or last minute things come up, we can do them without a big financial strain and not having to put them on a credit card or having to borrow money from someone, and we never have to worry about when or how we will pay it off.

So what is everyone's motivation to read my book and follow the debt elimination plan? Everyone is different and their financial goals are different. Some of you just want to be able to take care of your family without having to watch every penny. Some people want to buy a house or nice car. Others want to travel or retire early. So what are your financial goals? Get a piece of paper and write down your financial goals. Why do you want to learn to handle money better? Where do you see yourself in 5 years? Ten years? Twenty years? No really, get a piece of paper. Write down your short term goals of 2 to 3 years. Is this simply getting out of debt? A newer car? Just being able to pay bills every month and not have to worry about it? Whatever it is, write it down. Underneath of that, write down your financial goals for 5 to 10 years from now. Is this a new or a "fun" car? Is this a big family vacation all paid for? Is it buying your son or daughter their first car? Whatever it is, write this down too. Now what about 15 to 20 years from now. Is this simply living comfortably and never having to worry about bills or money? Do you want to retire a millionaire? (Yes this IS possible!) Do you want to be able to give to charity or simply give to those in need? Do you want to be able to pay for college for your young child or give them the down payment for a house? Whatever this long term goal is – WRITE IT DOWN! Make sure your goals are realistic. Don't write down that in 5 years I want to be a millionaire when you currently are buried in debt and make barely over minimum wage. Your 5 year goals should be simple like, pay off all credit cards, or take kids on a completely paid for vacation. Your long term goals can be bigger! Retire early. Pay off the house. Buy a Corvette! (can you tell I like cars?) Dream big here!!! Again, write down your goals for 5 years, 10 years and long term. If you want a classic car or motorcycle, for example, find a picture of what you want put it on this paper with your written goals. Don't be afraid to dream BIG! What can your life really look like in the future?

Keep this piece of paper in a spot you will see it often and if something else comes up that you really want, write it down. Did you just hear about someone riding across the country on a motorcycle or in a motorhome and want to do that? Add it to your long term goals. When you do have your financial house in order, this list can become like your bucket list where you can cross things off as you get them or do them! While I do have a "bucket list" for finances and it helps keep me motivated and reminds me of what I'm working for, the biggest gift to me is just not having to worry every month or every week. Just knowing things will be all right even when they don't go exactly to plan. Or as The Motley Fool put it:

> "Financial independence is not a set point or a single goal (although it is often most closely associated with retirement). It means having the freedom — the financial breathing room — to pursue your dreams and live at least part of your life exactly the way you want to at every step along the way"

Your future can be bright. I won't lie and say this will be easy. At times it's down right hard. You may think that this will never work, or that it will take forever. There are no quick fixes for building your long term financial health. But, if you take the time and do things right and stick to the plan, the rewards in the end are worth it. The times when your kids want to go somewhere or do something special and you can say "sure!" instead of "I'm sorry, we just can't right now". It's a great feeling!!!

CHAPTER 2

WHERE DO I START?

For most people their biggest purchase of their lives is their home. They save up all they can and look at several houses before they even think about making a commitment. They start thinking about what type of house they want. Is it a one story ranch, or a larger two story? Will it have a basement? Is the basement going to be extra living space or just storage or laundry area? Finally when they find a house they like they think about many factors and do research on the neighborhood and sometimes the schools in the area etc. This is not a small decision or one most people jump into quickly. It takes planning of what the future may look like. Will they be having children? Are there extra bedrooms for their future children? Is there a place to make a playroom? Or, are their children grown and now they don't need all the extra space? Overall buying a house takes a lot of research and planning and looking into the future to make sure this house will be what is needed for the long term. Most people understand this commitment when buying a house and probably get lots of advice before making any decisions.

When a person or couple finally make a decision on the house they really want, they get an inspection of the house. One of the main things that gets looked at during the inspection is the foundation. While most people may not know the ins and outs of building a house, they understand that the foundation is key to a good, long lasting house. If the foundation is not sturdy and able to withstand the pressure of holding a house up for years to come there will be problems. Big, EXPENSIVE problems, or the house may just fall to the ground.

So what about when you are building your financial house? As stated most people do a lot of work and research when looking for a house to live in, but do you think about your financial house? Do you think about how to build it? Do you think about how good the foundation is? Do you think about what it looks like? Or better yet what it SHOULD look like?

I know most of you right now are either shaking your head no or giving me a confused look because you have never really thought of it before. Most people say things like: "I save when I can" or "I have a savings account" (even though there may not be much in it). Some even say "I own some stocks" or "I have a 401k", yet most people don't even know how much is in each of these accounts or what they are invested in. These are all good, but are you really building a good financial foundation and then saving for the future and retirement? Is your financial house secure or would one storm/emergency topple your house to the ground?

When building a house or a building there are several different blueprints. There is the basic blueprints of the rooms that include where the walls are and how big each room will be. Yet, there are also several other layers of blueprints. There are electrical blueprints that show where all the wires will be and the outlets go. There are plumbing blueprints to show where all the pipes go and how they will flow in and out of the house. There are blueprints to show where all the heating and air vents will go and all these blueprints have to be able to work together.

So, where do we start or what are the blueprints to build your financial house?

I like to remember the steps or layers of blueprints to building a strong financial house by an acronym of something that every good house needs, BEDS!

B - Budget

E - Emergency Fund

D - Debt Elimination

S - Save/Invest

CHAPTER 3

THE "B" WORD

There is a word that starts with B, that when said, many people react to..

Some people may cringe or get a physical pain in their stomachs or heads. Others may simply roll their eyes or give dirty looks. Others simply get mad when they hear it and walk away to get away from the person who said it. When its first brought up this word can be a bad word in many households. That word is BUDGET! (What did you think I was going to say? This is a financial book isn't it?) When I first put our family on a budget (notice I didn't say "we" got on a budget, I said I PUT us on a budget) it was a bad word. One that meant I was probably going to say we couldn't spend some money or I was yelling because we went over-budget. When "budget" was brought up my wife had several reactions. She would give me that look, then roll her eyes, then tune out and many times just did or got what she wanted anyway. That's because we hadn't sat and talked and I didn't include her in the budgeting process. I hadn't talked to her about the "why" we needed to be on a budget and what a budget could do for our family. Don't make this a bad word in your household. Sit down and talk about your why and what a budget can do for your family. Make this a good word by saying what the budget CAN do for you and what IS in the budget. You must both be on the same page for a budget to really work and to really build your financial house strong. You must sit down and be totally honest and open about your financial situation. What credit cards or other debts you have and how much you owe on each. You also need to be open about how much you really make. I know married couples who can't tell me what the other person brings home or what deductions come out of their partners paycheck. You have to know what you are up against before you can plan your attack on how to beat it. You can't get to the finish line if you don't know where the start is.

So, When building your financial house the first, main blueprint is a budget. *A written budget every month that includes all of your income and expenses and where EVERY dollar will go for the month.* Every dollar should be accounted for on your budget. We will discuss where any extra money after bills are paid should go later on. You must establish your budget and get it fine tuned before you can move on to the other layers of blueprints and really building your financial house. The main blueprint must be right for the other layers of blueprints to flow together correctly.

If you were building a new house would you want the builder to come to you with just an idea in his head of what they are going to build or a scratch paper with a not to scale drawing on it and say: "we're going to put a couple bedrooms over here and I'm sure there will be a bathroom somewhere by the bedroom. The kitchen will be over here and I'm sure we will put a dishwasher and a stove in it, but I really don't know where yet." No way! If you are smart you would fire that builder right away! It's the same way with a budget. You can't say: "Well we have these bills to pay, and I'm sure we will eat out every week or so and the car will need gas, but I really don't know how much that will be". If you try to build your financial house this way it will have problems just like the house that builder was going to build.

Another way to think about this is that you are a coach and your family is your team. A good coach comes into every game with a good game plan. In this case the game plan is your budget and the opponent is your bills. A good coach will look at the opponent and see how he can minimize their strengths and expose their weaknesses along with bringing out the strengths of his own team. In this case your star player is your income and you put it up against their main players which are your bills and debts. You write down all their "players" (your bills you owe) and match them up against part of your income. Hopefully in the end your income wins out.

You must also try to minimize "unforced errors" or turnovers, which would be extra spending outside of the budget.

To start a budget you must know as close as possible what money is coming in and what your bills and expenses really are. The first month or maybe two, your budget probably won't work out exactly as planned. It may not workout anywhere near how you planned. You will probably be surprised how much you really spend on some things. Unless you are really in tune with your bills and expenses this is normal. So, each month you change things based on your last month's actual spending, or what you should be spending, and any anticipated extra expenses you may have that month.

Most people know the main expenses:

Rent or mortgage

Power bill

Gas bill

Car payment

Etc.

But do you really know what you spend on other things?

Groceries

Eating out

Gas for your car

Household items

Fun or other?

These items along with extra spending are what can break your budget if you don't control them. The first month you may be WAY off on these expenses or possibly even forget a major one. Did you remember your cell phone? Do you give to church? What about car insurance? Do you have some extra money to just buy a drink or snack at work? So this may take a couple months to get right. Usually by the third month you have a pretty good grasp on what your real expenses are. On the next page is a sample of a budget. Notice the "extra" money at the bottom is added directly into the smallest debt payment, which in this example is Credit Card 1.

Income

Reg. Pay	-	$3050 (check A $800 twice a month, check B $725 twice a month)
Home Business	-	$200
Total Income	-	$3250

Main (fixed) Expenses –

Mortgage/Rent	-	$450
Car 1	-	$130
Car 2	-	$150
Insurance	-	$110
Gas Bill	-	$50
Water Bill	-	$75
Power Bill	-	$70
TV/Internet	-	$140
Cell Phones	-	$110
Church Giving	-	$100
Christmas Savings	-	$40
Allowances	-	$400
Total Main Expenses	-	$1825

Credit Cards/Other Bills:		Minimum	Balance
Credit Card 1	-	$20 + $200	$440
Credit Card 2	-	$35	$1100
Credit Card 3	-	$50	$2000
Doctor Bill 1	-	$50	$500
Doctor Bill 2	-	$50	$1500
Dentist Bill	-	$50	$500
Student Loan 1	-	$100	$7000
Student Loan 2	-	$150	$5400
Total CC and other bills minimums	-	$505	

Other Items/Envelopes		Total	Weekly Amount
Gas	-	$160	40+40+40+40
Groceries	-	$300	75+75+75+75
Eating out	-	$100	25+25+25+25
Household	-	$60	15+15+15+15
Clothing	-	$40	10+10+10+10
Fun/Rec		$40	10+10+10+10
Vacation fund		$20	5 + 5 + 5 + 5
Total Envelopes		$720	$180

Total Income	-	$3250
Total Expenses	-	$3050

Extra to pay to CC1 - $ 200

Let's go through each section and break it down a bit. The first section is income with all main income together. While some couples keep separate accounts and pay certain bills separate, I feel you should combine your main income no matter who makes how much. If you are a couple and living together or (preferably) married and sharing expenses, then your income is one also. If you are at the point where you are combining bills and paying them together then you should have one main account to work from. Even though I was hesitant with this at first, my wife, then girlfriend, had us combine accounts. We were living together and paying everything together, it only made sense to combine our accounts. So after a few months of living together we did get a joint account. This way there was no issues with one person not paying as much towards bills or even though at the time I made more money, that didn't mean I got more "extra" money. We had made the commitment to combine households physically, so we combined households financially also. This also gave transparency into our finances and how much we both actually took home. We had both of our incomes direct deposited into this account so no one could hide part of their income from the other.

The second part of the budget is the main or fixed expenses. These are expenses that will always be there, except for car payments and eventually house payment. You will always have to pay a power bill and cell phone bill etc. Yes you can move the car payments down to the next section if you want. I put these up top because many people have and will probably continue to have a car payment. If you are paying off debt or barely making ends meet, you should definitely just get a inexpensive, mode of transportation. You don't need a fancy/newer car and I feel most people buy cars that are too expensive for their overall income and this is one of the main factors that keep people in debt and not saving. If you can afford it and have your other debts paid off or at least in control and are saving for retirement, I'm not totally against a small manageable car payment as long as your total car payments do not exceed 5-7% of your take home pay. As I'm writing this the average car payment is over $500 a month and studies now show that over 7 million Americans are at least 90 days late on their car payment. The easiest way to not be late on a car payment is to not have one. Our goal was to only have one car payment at a time and pay one off before we need another one. If you get a vehicle with a manageable payment on a 4 year loan, and then when that's paid off you get another vehicle with a 4 year loan, you would only have to keep cars 8 years before you could get a new one. OR, what if you kept the 4 year loan cycle, but kept each vehicle for 9 years? You would have at a year in between with no car payments at all! What if you kept a car for ten years? Or what if you paid it off in 3 years? If you basically saved what you would have put towards a car payment for those extra years, you could have a great down payment next time or buy your next vehicle straight up and never have a car payment again!

There are a few other lines you don't always see in other people's budgets. One is church giving. If you are a member of a church and believe what they stand for and what they are doing in the community and world, I believe giving is important and we have continued to give throughout our whole debt elimination plan. As our income has gone up and debt has gotten paid off, we have raised our giving and help out financially when we can with special projects at church. I believe in the vision of our church and am glad to help out where we can financially.

The second line you probably won't see in most "financial experts" budget plans is "Christmas Savings". This can also be called gift savings and be used for birthdays or anniversaries also. This is a big pet peeve of mine, people blowing their budgets or bringing out the credit cards to pay for Christmas gifts. Christmas is NOT a surprise. It's the same time every year and you do the same thing every year, spend money. This should be a no brainer to be added into the budget. In the budget shown they are putting in just $10 a week into Christmas savings. This will give them over $500 to use each year for Christmas gifts or for birthdays. While if you just buy for your immediate family or a small family this is a really good amount, but if you have a large family and buy gifts for everyone, this may not seem like much. Hopefully your family will understand that you are on a financial journey and that for possibly a few years the gifts won't be real expensive, but will be thoughtful. If they get upset or can't understand this, then they don't get the real reason for the season and to be honest will just have to get over it. Then when your debts are paid off you can splurge and give those closest to you even better presents in the future.

Christmas savings can be put into an envelope (as long as you don't get tempted to raid it if things get tight. Then you will have to break the budget for Christmas). We put ours in a separate savings account with automatic transfers into it each week. This can be set up at your local bank or usually even on line. This way you are saving money each week and don't even have to think about it. This should be separate from your emergency fund savings. This way you are not tempted to use just a little more for Christmas. Your emergency fund is for just that, EMERGENCIES. Not, for wanting to buy some extra presents at Christmas or anything else. If you are lucky the emergency fund will sit there and not be touched for a long time. A little trick we used for the Christmas savings was each debt we got paid off, we put in an extra dollar or two a week into it. An extra dollar a week is an extra $50 a year to spend on presents. This helped show us and the kids that things were getting better and would continue to get better, we just needed to keep going on our Debt Elimination Plan to get to even better times.

The last line on this part of the budget is "allowances". I believe we all need a little spending money each month for whatever we want. This should not be a large chunk of the budget. Just a little bit to do whatever you want with. My wife likes to go to Starbucks. While she can't get this every day, she can get maybe one a week. I use mine for drinks or snacks at work and sometimes eating out for lunch. This budget has $400 for "allowances" so basically $50 a week for each person. That's a pretty good amount of "extras". If needed can this be adjusted to $20 each a week? This would give more at the end of the budget that could be put straight towards your debt and your debts would get paid even quicker. Then when you are debt free you can raise this back up. Whatever amount it is, the amount should be agreed upon between the two of you and should be the same for both partners no matter who makes more money. One well known financial person said that the money you get to spend should be based on the percentage of total income you bring into the household. Here is my response to her and those agreeing:

> "So... You are making say $60k a year and you meet someone who is working and going back to school but only making $20k right now. You join lives (move in together and/or get married) and heck even maybe have a child together. During this time the person making 60k a year gets 3 times the spending money (to do whatever they want with) than the other person? So you may get $120 a week and then your WIFE or HUSBAND gets $40? That's $480 a month to spend while the other gets $120?

That is NOT becoming a couple and sharing your life equally. Just because the other person's situation didn't turn out as well as your's at the moment, BUT they are good enough and you love them enough for them to become your partner in life then you become EQUAL partners financially! If you can't handle that, then you are not ready to be partners with that person."

You are both equals in the household and working on your debt elimination plan together. This was the situation for my wife and I when we started out. She was making a good amount less, but was going to school to better herself and to get a better job in the future. Do you think it would have been good for me to go to her and say, "well since you make less than me you get less spending money than me. You'll just have to make it work." If I said anything like that I'm pretty sure she wouldn't be my wife right now. Since then she graduated and now makes as much or more than me and in her line of work will most likely continue to make more than me. Now if one partner just isn't earning much money and isn't working to find a way to make more or even trying to find a job, in other words just being lazy, then there are other issues besides money you two need to work out. But if you are both going to work or school and trying to better yourself and your financial situation then you are equals. Just because you make more money doesn't entitle you to make more of the financial decisions. Again, you two must talk about the budget and be on the same page. If one person just comes up and says "this is what we are doing and how much you will get to spend", the other person probably won't be too engaged or want to follow the plan very well. This is when it becomes the "B" word. It's much easier when you both are working on this together. I started putting my wife and I on a budget. She amused me for the most part and followed it usually. Then here and there extra charges on the account started popping up. I would then just get mad and tell her not to charge anything else. This way of managing the financial house didn't work too well. I finally sat down with her and talked through everything. I told her how much it was driving me crazy to be this far in debt and showed her where we were. I also talked with her about where I wanted to be and what we could do as a family if we didn't have all this debt to pay every month and what we needed to do to get there. She agreed to help stay on budget better and I agreed to not get so upset if one little extra charge showed up on the account every once in awhile. As things went along and she saw the debts getting paid off she was more and more engaged and on the plan. During one of our talks about the budget and how it was going, she was the one that suggested we lower our allowance each pay period. We then agreed and we had even more towards our smallest debt. It is crucial to both be on board with money.

If only one of you is making and sticking to the budget, it's like trying to swim out to sea with the waves hitting you every 3 seconds. You swim a few feet and get thrown back 2 feet. Then you swim 3 more feet and get thrown back 2 to 3 feet. Then every once in a while a big wave comes and you struggle to swim a few feet and get knocked back 10 feet. You will never get anywhere that way. When both partners in a relationship are on board with the budget it's more like having a boat. At first it may be a rowboat, but you are both paddling. Sure every once in a while you will get pushed back a bit by the waves, but eventually as debt gets eliminated, that row boat gets a small motor. Then you chug along a little better and fight through the waves a bit easier. Then eventually as more and more debt gets paid off you get a speed boat and fly right through the waves with very little resistance. Swimming against waves by yourself is hard and takes a long time and lots of energy and you still probably won't get very far and if you keep doing it for too long you may just get tired and drown. One partner building your financial house with the other not helping is the same and can be mentally draining at times. Both partners rowing together is much easier and will get you into the speedboat much faster. Then the fun begins where you get to figure out where all the extra money goes. Do you want new furniture? Do you want to take a vacation? What could you do with all the money going towards debt right now?

The next section is credit cards and other bills. These are the bills you want to ELIMINATE! The goal is to eventually not have this section of the budget at all. These include credit cards, doctor bills, student loans and any other bills that can be paid off and gone forever. As said above, car loans can also be here but I feel these others are more important to get rid of for good. Once things like credit cards and student loans are paid off, they can be gone forever. You will never need another credit card as long as your financial house is built correctly. This is why I call it a debt ELIMINATION plan (DEP) and not a debt reduction plan. I don't want you to just reduce your debt I want you to ELIMINATE it. Get rid of it and NEVER have to deal with it again. Paying that last payment on a bill is a great feeling. Paying the last payment on that credit card or student loan that you have had for YEARS is so uplifting. You can physically feel the weight being lifted off of you. You can even have a small celebration each time you pay one off. Heck, bake a cake with the name of the company you just paid off and cut right through it! It will feel THAT good! On these debts I also like to put the balance of each in this section. This helps you see how they are going down each month and also lets you see what debt you will be going after next. You start with the smallest debt and get it knocked out and then go to the next smallest. We will get into why you should start with the smallest debt later in the Debt Elimination chapter.

The next section of the budget is other expenses/envelopes. These are the basic needs to run a household and budgeting/ saving for other things that will be needed. When doing this part of the budget and trying to make sure we didn't go over budget on a certain category each week, we use cash and the envelope system. We took the budgeted money each week for each category and put cash in an envelope. (and no you don't have to buy a special "envelope system". While these are nice and definitely hold up better. To start out go to the store and spend less than $3 on a box of the small envelopes.

They fit bills perfectly and you will have extras to replace old, worn out ones with.) Your envelopes may be slightly different but we used categories: Grocery, gas (for cars), eating out, household, fun/rec, and vacation fund. Many people also have an envelope for upcoming things like oil changes or even car repairs. Our eating out, fun and rec and vacation fund envelopes were VERY small parts of the budget. Of course vacation fund is one that can be eliminated if needed. Using the vacation fund envelope gave us something to look forward to. It was basically enough to spend a week end somewhere once or twice a year or some money to have a day trip somewhere. Again, nothing big or fancy, just a reward for working so hard on the rest of our financial house and giving the kids a little something to enjoy since we were saying no to a lot of things during this time. By using cash in the envelopes if the money wasn't there, you didn't get it or go over budget. Even using a debit card (NEVER use a credit card) if you got a bit more at the grocery store than you thought it's too easy to just use the card and go over your budget. Eating out you HAD to watch what you ordered and the price and had to factor in what tax and tip would be. You can't go over or it comes out of your allowances. Using cash makes you pay attention to what you are getting and only getting what you really need. With the fun and rec envelope there was about enough going in there for us to see a movie once every month or two. If there wasn't enough there, we didn't do it and we didn't get popcorn and soda at the theater either unless we had enough in the envelope or one of us was willing to use our allowance to buy snacks. We got really good at finding free entertainment around our town. There were free kids movies about once a month. Free music in parks around town and lots of kid activities at the local libraries. Check your town or city's web site or local paper for free fun events!

As you will see on the budget there is a total monthly amount for each of these expenses, then I have separated these by weekly amount. This is for a couple different reasons. First you are not going to have an extra $700 at the beginning of the month to put it all into envelopes, unless you both get paid monthly at the same time. Also, by just putting in an amount each week, this helps you stay on budget a little better. The first week you only have a certain amount to buy groceries or go out to eat. If you spend the whole monthly amount the first week, you can't do anything else the rest of the month. By putting in cash weekly, you can go out to eat each week, or buy groceries each week. If you spend the whole grocery budget the first week and then it's the last week and somehow you ran out of food, you are out of luck. So this just helps you spread out your budget a little better so you don't overspend for the month.

The last part of the budget shows how much extra you can put towards building the emergency fund or towards the smallest debt. (We will talk about the emergency fund later on also.) You add up all of your income, then minus all three sections of expenses. This leaves you with the extra that you automatically put towards one of those. In this example the couple already had their starter emergency fund in place, so any extra goes to the smallest debt, which you will see is CC1 and has the minimum payment of $20 plus $200 which is the extra available in this budget. This is NOT extra to fudge other parts of the budget like eating out or allowances. It goes directly to the smallest debt.

CHAPTER 4

BUDGET PART II

S o it's the third month, you now know pretty much what you spend on each category each month, and you redo your budget to what you are really spending and your budget comes up with very little extra or even negative. There just isn't enough money for the month. This can be a HUGE realization that you are living beyond your means. There are 2 major ways to solve this. One is cut out some of the non-essential items or scale them back. Is there a gym membership that you don't use or don't need (if its summer or nice weather in your area most of the year, go outside and do your work out). You may not be able to have any extra "fun" money (no vacation fund or fun and rec) or scale your allowances way down. What does your grocery money look like? Do you buy some less expensive items or are you still cooking steak every week and buying chips and snacks all the time? Are you making the most of leftovers? Many times its cheaper to make a bigger portion of a meal to eat the next day than it is to make a whole new meal. One of our biggest cut backs when we started our budget was eating out. We LOVE to eat out. I still remember the moment when I knew we had a problem. We usually ate out every Sunday after church. We went to a nice place, ordered appetizers and drinks for all of us (just ordering water for 4 people can cut your bill by $10 or more!).

The bill came and after tip the total bill for our family was over $90! What? We just dropped almost $100 for lunch and it wasn't a special occasion???? That part of our spending had to be cut back so we could pay down debt. We still ate out, but definitely not as frequently and not at as expensive places as before. We also started to use cash so we watched what we ordered a lot more.

Is there a bill you can eliminate? Cable or Satellite TV? This can be a BIG expense that is not really a must have. Yes this may hurt to not have 160 channels at your fingertips, but if you have debt or can't make the budget work this is a great way to save some good money quick. For something to watch, get Netflix or Hulu while you are building or fixing your financial house and when things get better financially make this one of your rewards to get back later. What about internet? Do you HAVE to have this? Can you go to the library and use their computers or free wifi? If you basically just use internet to play games or go on social media, this is most likely an expense you can eliminate especially if you have a cell phone plan with large amounts or unlimited data. Speaking of cell phone plans, have you shopped around lately? We were with the same company for many, many years and just never thought about leaving. One day when we were actually going to add a line to our account (wanting to give them more money) some customer service issues arose. We looked around and found a plan with more data, plus added an extra line and saved around $30 from our old bill. So again, some of these are things you can get back when your DEP is done. Make these things to look forward to, kind of like a reward. You may actually find that when it's all said and done that you don't really need these and may want to use this new extra money for other things like family vacations.

The second option to help your budget is to bring in more income. Can you or your partner/spouse work overtime or get a 2nd job? Can you work a few nights a week somewhere or deliver pizza? Can you babysit a couple nights a week? There are many ways to possibly make some extra money. Can you drive for Uber? I talked to a guy recently that drives for Uber as a 2nd job and said he can earn an extra $1000 a month on good months. Can you be a waiter or waitress somewhere when you aren't at your main job? Can you deliver newspapers in the morning? Are you creative? Can you make items others would want to buy and sell these on the internet? Just get out there and do whatever it takes to make some more money! While I know this may not be the thing you really want to do, just know it can be temporary and when debts get paid down you can cut this back or eventually eliminate it if you want, or you can use this as investing money in the future. What if you start making money doing something you enjoy, can you expand this and turn it into your dream job?

I feel almost everyone can cut back on expenses somewhere. Very few people are really living their lives bare bones. I was once talking to a single mother in her mid 20's who was going to school and working a part time job. I talked to her about budgeting and building an emergency fund and she told me there was no way she could save even $10 or $20 a week. The very next week her car was damaged at night in the parking lot of her apartment building. Then the next week she got a speeding ticket. I asked her how she was going to pay for those and she said, "I guess I'll have to find it somewhere". If she can "find" the money to even pay for the speeding ticket, she can "find" $10 a week to build her emergency fund and could have cut back already. If you build your foundation, the rest will come and be easier. There won't have to be any "finding" money somewhere, you will already have it. You will have to make some sacrifices now to reach your goals and live a better life for years to come.

CHAPTER 5

WHAT DOES YOUR FINANCIAL HOUSE LOOK LIKE?

We have talked about the first step in building your financial house is having a good foundation. To have a good foundation you must first have a plan or a blueprint of how you are going to get there, which with money is a written budget. Now let's talk about what we think about when we talk about building a financial house and what we think it looks like compared to what it should look like and what it really does look like now.

When we talk about houses many of us first think of one of two things, a one story ranch or a two story larger house.

While a one story ranch is great! Thinking long term and thinking big is good. Even if you are working on your ranch right now, don't be afraid to dream about your two story financial home for the future.

Since we are talking about dreaming big and looking towards the future, we may even think of a tall skyscraper reaching up to the sky. This is great and what we could and probably eventually should reach for.

But what should be our goal right now? And what does our financial house look like at this moment? The phrase when I started out my career in business was always "think outside the box". Even when thinking about our financial houses maybe we should think outside the box. Maybe it shouldn't look like a box at all. Maybe we should look at structures that were built thousands and thousands of years ago and are still standing and strong today. Maybe our financial house should look more like this.

A pyramid with a good strong base and foundation to hold the rest of our financial lives up!

Yet, what does most of our financial houses look more like?

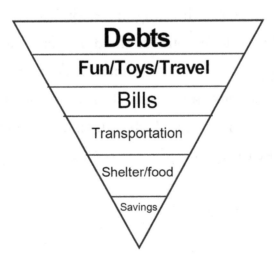

Does the second picture look like it has a sound foundation? Which one looks stronger and will continue to stand strong even when times are tough? If you keep adding to the top of the second one, eventually it's going to topple over and crush you. If the Egyptians tried to build their structures like the 2nd one, they would have never made it and would have never stood the test of time. Instead they had a good plan with a strong foundation to stand forever! Possibly once we have our financial pyramid in place, we can then build the sides out little by little until we have our own skyscraper, but we must start with a pyramid with a strong base.

CHAPTER 6

HOW DO WE GET THERE?

So how do we get do this? How do we turn our financial pyramid around the right way so it has a strong foundation? We will go step by step on how to build a good pyramid. Yes, we need to start with the foundation, but let's look at the top for a quick moment. This is fun/extras. This is your goals. What you like to do and want to achieve financially. Look back at what you wrote down on your piece of paper. Is your first goal to own your own home? What about long term?

Do you want to:

- Travel

- Own expensive/classic cars

- Retire early

- Own your own business

To get there let's go back to BEDS. We have talked about your budget. This is your first, basic blueprint, your map for each month on how you will achieve your goal. Hopefully after your budget is all laid out with your bills and expenses each month you have some left over. The next step to building that foundation is E, which is getting a starter emergency fund. Your emergency fund is like filling in the dirt around your basement or foundation. If there are gaps between your foundation walls and the ground, these walls may start to bow or bend and eventually will crumble. One little thing could bend your walls and start breaking down your foundation. You may hear the rule of 3 to 6 months of expenses for your emergency fund, but if you are weighed down with debt, you first need to get your starter emergency fund in place, which should range from $1000 to $1500. If you are renting your home or apartment, take the bus for transportation and have no children then $1000 is plenty to start out with. If you own your own home and car and have kids you may want to set aside $1500 to start out. Either way, $1500 should be your max starter emergency fund. Take the extra in your budget each week and instead of putting it towards your smallest debt, as shown in the previous budget, put this in a separate savings account until you build up this amount. I say put it in a savings account so this money is separate from the account you use for your daily and monthly expenses so you don't get the urge to use part of it each month. Your emergency fund is not part of your monthly budget to use, that's why it's called an EMERGENCY fund. The car breaks down, water heater at home goes out, your child breaks their arm and you have doctor bills. Those are unexpected emergencies, not that we just went over budget this week. Get this set and let it sit there and hopefully you never have to touch it. If it sits in your main account it's too easy to think that you have this extra money, so its ok to use, which it is not. Again, its an EMERGENCY fund. Not a "we spent a little extra this month" fund or we want to buy or do something fun. It's not a, we want new $150 shoes fund. It's not a, I want my hair done fund. It's not a we need a bigger TV fund. Its an EMERGENCY fund. A we don't touch it unless there is no other way, fund. Yet, you have to have an emergency fund because emergencies and unexpected bills will happen. It's not a matter of IF an emergency will come up, it's a matter of when.

Level 2 on the pyramid is basic needs. Many people say, "shouldn't you make sure basic needs are met before your emergency fund?" Yes, your VERY basic needs have to be met first. Basically food and shelter definitely come first before anything. But I am mainly talking about building your financial house in this book and I truly believe that having an emergency fund is THAT important to be put first and here is why. Without the emergency fund any little thing that happens can put your basic needs at risk and into a spiral downward for a long time. If you have made your budget to just get by for all your basic needs, then one thing can disrupt that and all of a sudden your basic needs are at risk. You have an emergency that must be taken care of, so you use the money you have budgeted for other things. Now you don't have the money for bills and rent. The next month you are trying to get caught up on last month's bills so you don't have enough to cover this month's. Another emergency hits and you dig further in the whole and can't pay rent again and now the landlord is talking about eviction and suddenly your basic needs are now in jeopardy. If your emergency fund is in place first, the one thing that happens is not as big of a deal. You use the emergency fund to take care of the emergency and move on. If you don't have enough for the very basic of your needs, then there is an issue. As we stated above, either cut expenses, or increase income. If these two don't help enough to take care of basic needs, then you seriously need to evaluate your expenses and life. If you are truly working every minute you can and can't make ends meet and have cut all expenses to bare bones, then look for help. Look at food banks or churches often have ways to help. While I believe everyone who is mentally and physically able should take care of themselves and their families for the most part, I know we all need some help every once in a while. If truly needed, there are places there to help you get over that hump in your financial life. If you truly can't take care of your basic needs of food, and shelter, go look for help. If you are going to school and need help until you are out, get help. Assistance of any kind is NOT your financial plan. It is help in those times when there is no other way. And I mean NO other way. This means you don't buy new things. If you NEED new clothes or shoes for you or your kids, you look at 2nd hand stores or garage sales. This is why I say emergency fund first. There is help for the basic needs when absolutely needed. When an emergency hits, there is rarely anyone there to offer you an extra several hundred dollars to take care of it. An emergency fund makes an emergency nothing but an inconvenience. You pay it, rebuild the emergency fund and move on.

So, yes the 2nd step is basic needs. Food, using enough to get what you need and a little extra. Truly covering your basic need of eating can be very inexpensive. While no one truly wants to live on ramen and peanut butter and jelly sandwiches, you may have to do close to this while you are building the emergency fund or on a real tight budget. Hopefully you can still eat a variety of foods and have other items once in a while, but it's all about moderation. You aren't buying steaks every week, you are buying $1 box of pasta and a $2 jar of sauce. Be smart on what you buy and make the most of leftovers.

Shelter – Again basic need to have a place to lay your head and take a shower etc. Yet, if you are not financially ready or able to afford a place of your own, you could get evicted or foreclosed on and then you are back to square 1. If you can't afford a place right now, can you stay with friends or family while you get your financial house in order? If so let them know your plan and possibly get an exit strategy in place. Let them know what your plan is and say "I just really need a place to stay for the next few months and will be out of here in 6 to 9 months at the latest and here's how I'm going to do it." Or, "I'm finishing school and as soon as I'm done I will look for a full time job. Even if it's not the perfect job that I want, I will graduate and hopefully have a job or a couple part time jobs if I have to, by next year at this time and will then get a place of my own." Also, make it beneficial for them too. Promise to wash the dishes and clean the kitchen once a week or cut the grass and shovel the snow when needed. Make yourself an asset to them and who knows, maybe they won't want you to leave so soon.

If you can afford a place of your own, get what you can

afford and be happy with it. For basic shelter this doesn't have to be an elaborate place or the best apartment around. What about having roommates to help split the rent? If you are single the answer is a definite yes. If you are a couple starting out, probably still yes. I rented a room off of a couple who bought a condo and wanted some extra income for a few years until I was financially stable enough to get my own place and they were able to afford the whole mortgage on their own a little easier. If you are a family with children, this is more tricky as you and your family have your own set of needs and the roommate will have their own. You would both have to respect everyone else and their needs and schedules to share a place, but this can be done as long as it's beneficial to everyone. Again, can you watch or babysit the kids from time to time? Can you run errands or take the kids to practice or meetings?

Step 2 can also include transportation. Can you take a bus to work and where you need to go? What about just walk or ride a bike while the weather is good? If not, can you financially handle a vehicle of your own? (Remember you will also have insurance to pay.) It is best to save your money and get a decent, inexpensive used car. If you think you can take on the responsibility of car payments, you can save that money each month and buy a car outright or at least put down a good down payment. Also when you pay a car off you can lower your insurance by only getting liability insurance in most states, when if you are paying on a loan for the car you must have full coverage. Again if you get a car you NEED an emergency fund. Older cars will have problems eventually, none will run forever. When a part breaks and you need a few hundred dollars to fix it, the money is there, no problem. If there is no emergency fund and there is a problem, you now have no vehicle and are back to square one with transportation and in deeper debt to get it fixed.

Yes, I said older/used car. If you are working on your debt elimination plan, and especially if you are still working on your basic needs, then there is no way you should have a new or close to new car. New cars are great! Something goes wrong, you take it back to the dealer and say fix it. Yet, obviously newer cars are much more expensive and if your credit isn't the best, your interest rate on a loan will be higher. I know a person who has a vehicle that is basically the same type of vehicle as mine, the same year and has more miles than mine. This person is paying over $100 more a month because of the interest rate she had to get. Also new cars lose value as soon as you drive them off the lot. You literally just lost several thousand dollars driving the car home from the dealership. Cars are normally NOT a good investment and should not be looked at as one.

It is much better to take a couple thousand dollars, or less if you can, and buy a decent used car for now. If this car can last even 2 to 3 years it's much better than having car payments stretching for years and years to come. Even at a modest $200 a month payment you are paying over $2,000 a year. I have seen loans advertised for up to 7 years now! Save up the money for a used car, pay for it outright and work on your debt elimination plan. Then hopefully in a few years when you NEED a different car, you will have the means to buy one or possibly get a bit better used car. Cars are one of the biggest things people overspend on. The average new car payment in America right now is more than my mortgage. That's INSANE! We all think we must have the newest, best looking, fastest car, when in reality, we need something to get us to work and possibly around town. I know college students who work part time and have thousands of dollars in student loans buying 1-2 year old cars and having hundreds of dollars in car payments every month. They are just digging themselves in deeper and deeper debt to where they won't be able to survive financially for many years to come. When you are working on building your financial house, a car is transportation and that is it. When you get debt paid off and your financial house built right this can be one of your goals. The joy of sitting in a new, or just slightly used car, and actually being able to afford it, is a great feeling. When the time is right you won't have to worry about the payments being too much anymore, just keep payments 5%-7% of your take home pay or less to make sure you have enough money to live the rest of your life and invest for the future.

I will also say it's an even greater feeling to walk into a car dealership and tell them what you want instead of them telling you "what they can do for you". Be educated when you walk in. If you need to get a loan for the car, again when your financial house is in order and you can afford it, know your numbers. Know your credit score. Know what you can afford and stick to that number. Do some research and know what interest rates are at other places. Check your local credit union as I have found they usually have better rates than local banks. I walked in to buy my last vehicle with a nice down payment. I had researched online and found the vehicle I wanted. I walked in and said this is what I found on interest rates, can you match it and they did. It was also good that my wife and I played "good cop/bad cop". We have done this unintentionally before buying cars because they like to think you are stupid and come back with deals WAY out of your price range and it takes you hours to get them to the deal that you know you can get anyway. So this time my wife wasn't there, she was at work. So when we started talking about price I called her. We had discussed before what price we wanted to get the vehicle for. They of course told us they couldn't go as low as we wanted. When I called her, she and I came to an agreement of what we wanted to pay and that was it. I told the dealer and he at first said he couldn't go that low even though we weren't asking for that much off of what they were asking. My wife finally said, "that is how much I think we should pay and if they aren't willing to take that then we will keep looking". I shook my head at the dealer and told him my wife said I can't spend more than this amount. If you can't do that I have to leave. Of course he had to go talk to someone else who then came over and talked to me. He again talked to me about pricing and how the number he gave me earlier was as low as they could go. I again told him that we would be buying a car in the next month or so one way or another and that my wife said that we get it for this amount or I have to leave and we keep looking. He kind of shook his head and talked about how much they have in the vehicle. I looked at him and said our credit is great, I have a cashier's check for a good down payment that I'm ready to sign over to you. I'm ready to sign the papers today, but I can't walk out of here paying more than this certain amount. He gave me the look (you know the one like it's physically painful for him to go any lower) and said "let me go look at the numbers again". He came back a few minutes later and gave us the deal we asked for. Being informed of our credit scores, the interest rate we could get and most of all not being in a spot where we HAD to buy a car, but letting them know we would be buying a car from someone soon gave us the leverage we needed. We weren't trying to way undercut them, but did want to get a good deal. I wasn't being mean or nasty about it, just, with the help of my wife, stood my ground. Also, buying a car if you are a couple is a family decision. I have heard about people coming home with new cars and the other person having no idea about it! Talk to your partner about any financial decision, especially one that is thousands and thousands of dollars. Agree on what you want and how much you want to spend and stick to it. Any differences in the agreed amount need to be discussed and agreed upon by both partners.

Although my last experience overall was a good one, I have several stories about car dealers, including how one guy wasted a whole day of ours after I told him there was no way he could get us in the new car he was showing us (when we went there looking at one of their used cars) for what we wanted to pay. He assured me he could and after going back and forth several times I eventually heard the "money guy" laughing and saying "no, there is no way I can sell that car for that". This was 4 hours AFTER I told the guy the same thing.

I even tried the "lay cash on the desk to get the deal done" trick once. We went in and tried to buy a used car with cash and I was not nice about it. We were trying to get a decent deal on the car and after checking the car out and test driving it, decided we wanted it even though there were some small issues with it. We went to the office and I said, this is the money we have, tax, title, license included take it or leave it. Of course the dealer got all defensive and said "I can't do it for that amount". I said "That's all we have. That's the deal. If you can't do it for that then I'm ready to leave". He again said there was no way he could do it for that amount, I said "OK let's go" grabbed the money that I had laid on his desk and walked out of his office. Luckily my wife was there who is usually the calmer head between the two of us. She apologized to the man and eventually pretty much got the deal we wanted. Yes it took an hour or so, but we got it. So my point of this story is to be firm, but not nasty about the transaction. If you are buying at a dealer know that they are trying to make as much money as possible too, like you are trying to save as much money as possible, so negotiations are what will happen and hopefully you will meet somewhere in the middle. Don't get pushed into a deal you really don't want, or can't afford. There first offer is almost never their best offer. Very few places say take it or leave it without going back and forth a bit and don't get into a deal you don't want or really can't afford. But I learned my lesson as being nasty and not negotiating got me nowhere.

CHAPTER 7

DEBT ELIMINATION

The next part of BEDS is D for Debt Elimination. This is the biggest and hardest step for most of us. But once its gone, it can be gone forever! You can then use your money to enjoy life and build wealth.

So, I have always been pretty good with finances. I have always saved money since the time I started getting money for birthdays and holidays. Then as a pre-teen or early teenager I started cutting grass and grew this into a small business. I started out helping cut our own yard. Then my grandparents were nice enough to let me cut their yard and paid me a bit (and there was always ice cream and cookies at the grandparents' houses when I was done). Then a friend of my mom's needed her grass cut. With help from my dad, within a couple years I was making up to a couple hundred dollars a week as a teenager working part time. Back then I think minimum wage was around $5 an hour, so this was a pretty decent amount, especially when I made my own hours. Most of the time I worked hard a couple days a week and had the rest of the week free. I saved a good chunk of that money and bought my first car with cash a couple months before I was 16. The car was 10 years old when I bought it and ended up lasting me 7 years when I sold it for just $200 less than I paid for it. It had things break on it and repairs that it needed and since I had money saved, (basically a teenage emergency fund) this was not a problem. Having a dad and uncle that could work on cars back then helped too. Plus I learned a thing or two. I remember changing headlights, an alternator and a turn signal switch, and changing my own oil. My dad and I changed the brakes and I think the belts on the car and did several other small repairs.

Then college came and of course they pushed credit cards down our throats with free T-shirts or other items. So I signed up for a couple cards and since I had them, I started using it here and there when I didn't want to use all my extra money. Then I had student loans while my credit cards slowly crept up. Then, several years later, I met the woman who later became my wife. She had 2 children and of course I wanted to be a fun guy to make them like me more and accept me into their family. We ate out at restaurants a lot and did a lot of fun things. The winter before we got married we all went on a week long ski trip to Colorado! It was amazing and I will never forget it. I will also never forget the cost as we estimated that this trip in total was almost $8,000!!! For one week! A good portion of that on credit cards. Again I have no problem with people taking these trips and spending $8000, if they can afford it. By "afford it" I mean pay for it and not use credit cards. At the time, we couldn't really "afford it" and it took YEARS to pay that off.

This continued for a while, including our honeymoon, again part on credit card. Joining households I figured that she was on her own, I was on my own, combining households and incomes would mean we have more money right? Wrong! Somehow we still didn't have extra money. The credit cards kept creeping up and she finished school and now had her student loans to pay also. My wake up call was while doing our taxes one year. My wife had gotten a promotion early in the tax year and we made decent money that year, yet had no extra money because we were paying on so much debt and living above our means. I was yelling about money constantly and griping about every purchase made. I finally had enough and we quit using credit cards. This was great, but we still had no extra money. We had enough for bills and that was it, because we were overspending. We finally got on a written budget and started our own debt elimination plan by attacking the debts one by one. At first my wife was still not happy with me griping about every purchase, so we sat down and talked. We talked about how we couldn't keep living like this and working our tails off and not enjoying any of it. We talked about where we wanted to be with money and all the things we could do if we weren't paying hundreds and hundreds of dollars every month on debt. I also promised to back off and not gripe about every little purchase once debt was paid down. I think that alone convinced her to help work the plan.

We started paying down debt one by one. We had some doctor's bills that we paid first since they were small and then attacked the credit cards one by one. Again, start with the smallest debt first. Pay minimum payments on all other debts and put any extra you can spare in your budget to the smallest debt no matter the interest rates. Then when you get this paid off, you can roll over the payment you were making on this one and add it to the minimum payment on the next smallest. 100% of the payment from the first debt will go to principle and pay it down! Take a look at the example of a DEP, Debt Elimination Plan, below.

Debt 1 - $300

Debt 2 - $1000 - Minimum payment $50

Debt 3 - $1500 - Minimum payment $50

You find after doing your budget that you can put $100 a month towards the first debt. Say this is a doctor bill with no interest so it takes 3 months to knock out. The next month you start on debt 2 and start paying $150 a month. (The $100 a month you were paying on the first debt plus the $50 minimum of debt 2) Now instead of this taking over 17 months to pay off with only minimum payments, it's paid off in less than 9 months! You move on to debt 3 which is now down to about $1200 after payments and interest added for the last 9 months. You now have the $150 you were paying on the last debt, plus the $50 minimum payment you were already paying added together for $200 each month going towards this debt and its gone in just over SIX MONTHS!!! Instead of taking another 2 years of just paying minimum payments on this debt alone, it is now all gone in less than a year and a half! The key is to write the budget, stick to it and put everything possible towards debt.

People always ask: "Shouldn't you start paying more on the one with the highest interest rate?" The short answer is no. While mathematically, yes this would save you a little bit of money in the long run and make your time paying debt slightly shorter, winning with money isn't all about math, at least the paying off debt part. Winning with money is about behavior and while working your DEP it's about getting those small wins to keep motivated. It feels SO much better to knock out and eliminate a couple small debts and roll over those payments into the next smallest debt and build the total amount you can pay on those debts. When you are paying on one large debt for a long time it's very easy to become discouraged and not want to continue. The smaller debts also just sit there, many times making very little head way since the monthly payments are so small and mostly get eaten up by interest charges anyway.

A new study from the Harvard Business Review now backs this way of thinking up. It states:

> "Our research suggests that people are more motivated to get out of debt not only by concentrating on one account but also by beginning with the smallest."

It also says:

> "...our findings would argue against pooling debts into a single larger one as this can actually be demotivating and could slow progress in

repayment. "Pay the smallest debt first" is a straight forward strategy that can be easily communicated and easily applied—and that's sorely needed by millions of American credit card users."

As I said before, this isn't easy. Yes it takes time, but after its done, you are free from debt forever!!! I will tell you it's a great feeling to now have that extra money available. When you have the extra money, those situations that would have been a big issue and you would have had to figure out how you would handle them, now are not a problem at all. We had a situation recently where my wife's family had a family member get very sick and my wife had to travel out of state with about one day notice. She drove down there with family, but said she may have to fly back because of work issues. Before, when we were drowning in debt with no extra money this would have been a BIG issue. We would have had to dive into our emergency fund and put a big dent in that, that is if we even had one at the time (otherwise this would have probably been put on credit card and sat there adding interest to the debt). We would have taken months to build the emergency fund back up and then get back paying on debt and even though I knew she had to go to be with her family, I'm sure I would have griped or at least mumbled about the money.

It wasn't like that this time. We had most of the main debt paid off and a solid emergency fund, so I said, "OK, just tell me how much you spend and how much the plane ticket will be". I even said, "Here's an extra couple hundred dollars for meals and expenses". It was nothing for this to happen. Since we had the emergency fund set and had most of our debts paid off, this was nothing more than an inconvenience financially. We may have to wait an extra couple months to go on our next vacation or scale it back a bit, but that is it. My wife is very glad now that we got on the plan and I am way more relaxed about money. It was a very hard several years. We did very little extra. Our vacations were mostly family functions that we stayed at the family member's house and maybe took an extra day for a zoo or something. Yet we celebrated paying off all credit cards and doctor's bills (and my student loan) by going to Disney World and paying ALL of it up front! NO CREDIT CARDS! Now looking back on that trip we can just look at all the great times and memories of this truly a once in a lifetime trip for our girls, and NOT all the debt we now have to pay back from it.

As I'm writing this we had another mini emergency. The garage door opener broke and it was over $300 to fix it. Could we have lived without the garage door automatically going up and down? Sure we could have, but since we had built the emergency fund and had built a strong foundation for our financial house, this too was just an inconvenience. Within a month, two situations that would have been financially devastating just a few years ago, now are not major issues. It still pains me to spend money on things like a new garage door opener, but now I get over it much quicker. I think it was about a minute of me thinking about everything else I could do with that $300 or how much quicker our car would be paid off, and then it was over. We paid it and moved on! It's a great feeling. Keep working on your debt elimination plan and you too can turn emergencies into inconveniences!

CHAPTER 8

INSURANCE

So we all know that if we drive we must have car insurance. It's the law plus it can be financially devastating if you are in an accident, especially if it's your fault and the other person is hurt. The medical bills could be in the hundreds of thousands of dollars. Health insurance is another that I think most of us agree is a must. Medical bills can drain you or truly put you in financial ruins if there has to be a stay in a hospital or a surgery.

There's another insurance that is a must if you have a family, life insurance. Many people think life insurance is for old people, when in reality it's almost just the opposite. Life insurance is for people who have other people who depend on their income. If you are older and have no debt and no one is dependent on you and your income, you really don't need life insurance. It's nice to have or at least have enough money to pay for expenses in case you pass away, but not really necessary. Even if you are retired with a nice nest egg that can pay for anything you owe and any expenses then you don't need life insurance at all. If you are single, have no kids or anyone who depends on you financially and have no real debts then you also don't have to have life insurance.

Now, if you have children or even just a spouse that

depends on your income then you must have life insurance. Would your wife be able to pay all the bills if you passed? Would your children be able to still attend college if you passed? Do you really want the added pressure on your family of not having any money, and possibly new medical bills from whatever happened to you along with the grief of you not being there? There are several methods out there about how much life insurance you need. Some people simply say 10 to 20 times your annual pay. I've heard people say that they have enough to pay off all debts and after that their spouses income can cover the normal expenses. There is also what is called the DIME method.

D - Debt

I - Income replacement

M - Mortgage

E - Education

Each of you should have enough to pay off all debt including mortgage, replace your income for as long as needed (the person I talked to about this recommended until the children are 18 and can support themselves) and enough to pay for all children's upcoming education or college.

So, if you owe $150,000 on everything including the house.

You make $50k a year and have a child who is 12 and estimate it will cost $20k a year for college, here's the math.

Debt + 6 yrs income + 4 yrs of college =

150,000 + 300,000 + 80,000 = 530,000

You could also bump income up until the child is out of college so add another 4 years or 200k. This would bring it up to 730,000 of coverage.

No matter what method you use, the main thing is to not put a burden on your family and hopefully set them up financially to be ok without you. I keep seeing over and over again posts on social media where people set up donation or go fund me pages to help out a family after a tragic accident took the life of one of the parents and now they have to basically beg other people to help with funeral expenses and to just live and take care of the child. All this could have been avoided if they just had life insurance. Make sure you get TERM life insurance. As this says you pay for life insurance for a certain "term" or amount of time, usually between 10 and 30 years. While after the term is up and you don't use it (which is the ultimate goal anyway) then you do lose the amount you paid for the insurance, but the premiums are much lower than other types of insurance. Another type of Insurance, usually called whole life, is basically investments with very high fees and many times they don't keep up with the market over the long term. These are also much more expensive each month than term life. Keep your insurance and investments separate. You will most likely need more insurance while you are younger and have debts and are building your financial house anyway. You will need the extra money that is the difference between the monthly payments on term life and other life insurance products. We were given the whole life insurance talk once. They made it sound awesome and truthfully I was close to signing up. Luckily I knew that at the time we didn't have the money to pay the monthly premium and I'm glad we didn't as it would have put us in even more debt and put our DEP way behind when we finally got on a plan. After your debts are paid down you will eventually become what is called "self insured" where you can cover all costs needed and have extra for your family with what you have saved and invested in your life.

CHAPTER 9

SAVINGS AND
INVESTING

So you are now debt free and wondering where to go from here? That brings us to the "S" in BEDS, saving and investing for your future. Your next move is save approximately six months worth of expenses for your major emergency fund. As I said this is expenses, not your whole budget amount. This is just what you really need to pay all your needed expenses in case of a major emergency like you lose your job. So this would not include vacation savings or investing. This is just what you must have to keep your household running while things get figured out.

So, where should you keep this money? This should NOT be in stocks or other volatile investments. Why? Because if another financial crisis happens like in 2008, then you lose half of your emergency fund. If your emergency savings was invested in stocks in 2008 and you lost your job and needed this to live on, your emergency fund was just cut in half, and now instead of a 6 month emergency fund, you are down to 3 months. This needs to be kept safe so it's there when you need it, it's more of being self insured than an investment. While I'm not a fan of having this just sit in a savings account earning 0.0000002% interest, this should be in an account that you can get to the money within a few days tops and something safe. So no long term investing like a

CD or anything like that. (which CD's are not making much more in interest right now either, but that could change in the coming years.) There are a couple solutions to safe investing while getting a little better interest rate than a regular savings account. There are several online banks who are giving up to 2% or more interest on savings accounts. Another is a money market account. These are like savings accounts but let you take a limited number of withdrawals per year. Which since this is your major emergency fund, hopefully you won't be taking any out at all or at least only once or twice a year at most. These accounts also have a bit higher minimum balance requirement than typical savings account. So when you get to the point where you are ready to build your major emergency fund. Talk to your local bank and see what the balance requirements are. Overall Money market accounts are usually the best use of your money for your emergency fund. It's a bit higher interest rate, but also safe where you won't lose money.

LONG TERM INVESTING

As I stated at the beginning of this book, I mainly want to get you started on your journey to financial freedom. I want to help get your budget set and debts paid off. Yet, I also want to get you started in investing. You've heard the phrase "it takes money to make money". Well now that all debt is paid off, except for the house, you have that money to start really making money for the future. The next step to building wealth and investing for the long term is getting your retirement account(s) going. Your very first step, if your company has one, is your 401k. Most major employers have them and will match your contributions up to a certain percentage. Say If you put in 5% of your pay every check, the company will match this 5% and put that into your account also. So even if you invest in super conservative funds that make no return, you have doubled your money that you invested for the year!!! I like doing a 401k because the money comes out of your pay automatically before you even see it. It's not something you consciously have to take the money and invest in and you learn to live on the take home pay that you get. You pretty much forget that you make more money after a while and it's easy investing.

There are a couple types of 401k's. There is traditional where money is taken out of your paycheck pre-tax. This lowers your taxable income for the year, so you actually have less taxes coming out of your check, which can help with overall take home pay. When you do end up taking the money out after you retire, you will be taxed on all of the money you put in, and the gains that you have earned. So you will have to account for the taxes coming out of that money. So if you take $2000 out each week, you may only get $1500 to spend.

The other type is a Roth 401k. This takes money out AFTER taxes have been taken out. So you get taxed now on that money too and it qualifies as income in the current year. So your paycheck will be a bit less if you do a Roth 401k instead of a traditional 401k, but I believe its worth it.

For example if your taxable income is $1750 each check (approximately a $45,000 a year salary), getting paid every 2 weeks, and you put in 10% of that into your 401k. We'll say 20% of your pay taken out for taxes, you will take home $35 less each check if you do a Roth 401k instead of traditional.

Taxable income   - $1750
10% of $1750 invested (1750 - $175
x .10)
20% taxes on $175 ($175 x .2)   - $35

So why would you do a Roth 401k and take home less money? When you retire and take out the money you invested as a Roth 401k it is all TAX FREE, including all of the gains you have made in the investments. Look at the example below. This takes into account for only what you put in, it does not add in the company match, which usually goes into a traditional 401k and not Roth. This example also doesn't account for pay raises or additional contributions, so your actual total will probably be much higher. This is an example and tax rates are estimates and not actual tax rates.

I'm also using an 8% annual return on your money which is actually lower than the 20 year average return from the S&P 500.

Example

$175 x 26 checks a year - $4,550

$4,550 for 20 years - $91,000

8% return - $224,458

In 20 years you will have $224,458 TAX FREE! If you wait 25 years until you retire this then jumps to $362,776!!!

If you would then have to pay 20% taxes on the $362,776, the taxes taken out would be over $72,555! When if getting to keep the difference in your paycheck each time if you did a traditional or before tax investment, that would be about $35 a check. That $35 for the last 25 years you would have gotten less than $23,000 extra. So would you like to get $23,000 more in your check in 25 years or have an extra $72,000 in retirement? I'll take the $72,000!

(Yes your tax rate may be lower in retirement than when you are working, but if you are investing for the long term of 10-15 years or longer, you will most likely pay more in taxes and have less in retirement using a traditional 401k since you will be paying taxes on all money you invested AND all the investment gains.)

Once you have invested enough into your 401k to get the full company match there are other options you can look into. You can get an IRA or Roth IRA. Again I recommend the Roth as long as you qualify as there are income limits. With Roth IRA's you can also take out the money that you put in at any time without penalty. While I don't recommend taking money out of retirement accounts, it can act like an extra emergency fund if needed in case of major issues like an injury or other reason you would not be able to make money for more than 6 months. There are also single company stocks, mutual funds, Index funds and TONS of other options. Again, I will try to stay pretty basic but give you some information on some options below.

Single company stocks many times give you the freedom of investing smaller amounts at a time so you can sometimes put even $100 in each time. While I don't recommend this as you will usually have a trading fee each time you buy or sell a stock. Single company stocks are also the most volatile as they may go up or down drastically in a short time. If there is a true problem with a company it can go down and either never recover or take several years to come back up. If there is one quarter when their sales or earnings do not meet expectation these can fall by 10% or more within days. If you are going to start with single stocks, make sure you research the company and know it is a strong, good, long standing company and be warned that even if you think it's a good, long standing, reputable company, things can happen and you could lose all or most of your money. I would never put all of your extra money into one company stock. If you really want to do single stocks, pick a few good companies and split it around those, preferably in different sections of the market. You don't want to buy 2 or 3 companies all in the banking industry or all in the energy field. Maybe think about one company in banking, one in health care and one in energy for example. I have invested in very few single stocks in my life and they are a very small part of my overall portfolio. Of the single stocks I have done 2 have been my employer company stocks which have both been fortune 500 companies. Over the long term these have done decent, but have had many fluctuations. One has dropped almost 20% in less than a month. I believe this will come back up eventually, but it could take a couple years to recover fully and go back up. Of the other single stocks I have tried, only one has given decent returns. A couple have been losses for me including one that is currently over 40% down from when I bought it. This is in a growing industry, but this single company itself doesn't seem to be taking off, but we will see. It was on the cheaper side, so I am going to let it sit and see what happens.

Another way to go are index funds. While many investing professionals don't like these, I feel, especially for the beginning investor, that these are a great way to get into the market. You invest your money in a fund that is supposed to closely match the actual markets. You can do a fund that matches the Dow or the S&P 500, or one like the Russell 2000. These give you a way to invest in a large group of companies and they are easy to track for the beginning investor as every newspaper or news show that talks about money at all will have statistics on the Dow and S&P 500 and these are easily tracked on your stocks app on your phone. A good chunk of my portfolio is in index funds.

If you want to get more into investing there are thousands of ways to do it. One of the most common are mutual funds. Again you are picking a fund that has a group of stocks in it, so it is more diversified and usually less volatile than single stocks. You want a fund that has a long history of good returns. There are thousands of funds out there with several different types. While I look for growth and growth and income mutual funds, please do some research and look at the long term returns for each fund and compare those to other funds. Also, many mutual funds have a minimum investment that has to be made. While some are quite large at $5,000 to $10,000, there are many as low as $2,500 or even $1,000. Some funds also require you to keep the money in that fund for at least 6 months, so please read all the qualifications and rules for the fund.

My final thoughts on investing. Be in it for the long term. Unless you see a true, large, long term problem on the horizon in our economy, like the financial crisis of the late 2000's, then stay in the market. (did anyone really think people were going to be able to take out the subprime and interest only loans and magically be able to afford mortgage payments of several hundred dollars higher in a few short years when they were already maxed out on what they could afford already???) Also it has been shown that there has NEVER been a 20 year time period when the market has lost money. So if you are in it for the long term you are pretty much guaranteed to not lose money and have a very high possibility of gaining plenty.

Some people try to time the market and guess when stocks or a stock is going to gain and when it's going to lose. Timing the market is not easy and there have been studies on how most people lose their money by trying this. I have rarely moved stocks around or sold (or bought) because of what I thought the market was going to do. Overall I'm very glad I didn't as several times when I thought the market was ready to crash or at least go down, it hasn't and actually has gone up quite nicely in the time frame I thought all indications were showing a drop. There is a saying "It's not about timing the market, it's about time IN the market".

The other thing is if something like the financial crisis happens again and you do have your money heavily in stocks, don't take it all out. The stock market will, eventually recover. From the bottom of the stock market in 2008 to 2015 the market recovered and almost TRIPLED from its low and has kept going up since then, including breaking it's all time high over and over again. I have seen stories of people who even in the last few years still said "we lost all our money when the market crashed in 2008". My first question is why? They then say when it crashed they took it all out. If they would have left their money where it was and waited it out they would have gained it all back and much more. This is also why you keep your main emergency fund in safe, less volatile places and not all in the stocks. If you would have had your main emergency fund in the stock market at this point and lost your job, you would have also lost half of your emergency fund and would have been forced to take out what was left to just live. This is how you lose all of your money in a stock crash.

Overall I am a fan of the stock market and have made good returns from it and expect to in years to come. But I also know that it will drop at some point and while it hurts to see and know that you are losing money, I know eventually it will go back up to where it was and more. I don't try to guess its day to day or even week to week movement. I know at some point it will go down and at another point it will go up. I have listened to financial "experts" tell me when I should get out of the market or what months are better than others. There is a financial planner on our local radio that for several years has used the phrase "sell in May and go away". If I would have listened to him the first few years I heard him say this I would have missed out on double digit returns just in those few months. I have even read about silly things like how which team that wins the super bowl could tell you how the rest of the year will be with stocks. I also would have lost a good amount of money if I listened to some of them.

CHAPTER 10

FINAL THOUGHTS

When I was younger I loved playing sports. In my youth I don't think I had a week off between seasons and many times practice started for the next sport before the other was over. As I got older and the skills and other factors made me quit or cut back on most sports I started running. I started training for a 5k, which my first one I remember having to stop several times because I could barely breathe and my wife asked as I came by if I was ok as she saw the look on my face (like I was ready to die). Eventually I kept training and was able to keep doing better at 5ks. I then started training for and have done several half marathons. Now, I'm definitely not a fast runner or one of those runners that can run a 5k or more and be totally fine and look like they hadn't even run yet. I'm sweaty, I'm tired, and even though I'm never last, I'm certainly not one of the faster runners. But, running has has taught me a lot about life and about how to think about money.

First is to not worry about everyone else. In running there will always be someone faster or better than you. Unless you are one of the gifted few, you will probably never be first in a race like a 5k or half marathon. This has taught me that it's not about them, it's about me. When I run it's about how I feel and if I'm improving on my times and mainly that I'm just out there doing it. I can't think about the others running pretty much a sprint the whole race as I can never do that. I focus on my pace and my breathing and my time. It's the same with money, you have to focus on you. You can't look at your neighbors and their new cars and new clothes. You can't look at your friends or coworkers and think about all the vacations they are taking. Truthfully, many of them are broke and in so much debt that one little thing would throw their financial world into a downspin or they will simply have to work until they die to pay for all of it. You must focus on you and your race to financial freedom. Focus on your spending, your debt elimination plan and then your building wealth.

Second, winning with money is not a sprint, it's a marathon or in my case a half marathon. It won't be quick, it won't be easy and at times you will want to quit but it's a great feeling when you cross that finish line. Running 13 miles is not easy for me at all. Many times during the race I get a little over half way through and wonder if I'm going to make it to the end. Then by the time I cross the finish line I just want to sit down and not move or do anything, but then the feeling of accomplishment comes over me, energizes me and puts a smile on my face! It's a great feeling to be able to put my mind to something and even though I wasn't sure I'd make it at times, to finish what I set out to do. It's the same with winning with money and building your financial house the right way, it's a marathon. You must work at it and keep pushing through even during the hard times and times you don't think you can keep going. But in the end there is a great feeling of accomplishment and you can now put that smile on your face and live your life with the freedom you have always wanted.

I hope you have enjoyed my book. I hope that you will look at money differently now. Even if things are tough now, better days are on the horizon. You have to make the future better by taking steps now to make it that way, because no one else will do it for you. Build your financial house the right way by making a budget, building the emergency fund and paying off debts that you will never have to pay on again. Pay off the credit cards and cut them up. Don't rely on anyone else but you to be in charge of your future. Keep the paper with your goals and dreams on it where you can see it often. There will be times when it will feel like you will never achieve those dreams or that they are so far off that they aren't worth fighting for, but they are. The release of stress when you don't have to worry about money every day or where every little penny is going is amazing. It is like a ton of bricks are taken off your shoulders. As you pay down debt it's like a brick is taken off every once in a while. You feel a little better, it's a little easier walk and breath and before you know it more and more bricks fall off, until you can finally stand up straight with your head held high and take a deep breath. You have done it. You have won with money. You have built a strong financial house! You can invest for your future. You can take care of yourself, your family and your bills and have a little fun while you are at it. You can buy your kids the birthday and Christmas presents they want. You can upgrade your car or furniture in your house. You can go on a trip and not worry about how you are going to pay for it. It's an AMAZING feeling. Our big "we did it" trip was to Disney World. We had promised our girls that when we got things paid off and saved enough money we would go. We hadn't gone on any major vacations for several years so this was big for all of us. I truly can't even describe how I felt watching my girls get the royal treatment and get their hair done inside of Cinderella's Castle in Disney World and knowing it was all already paid for and we didn't have to worry about paying for it for years to come. We were just able to watch their smiling faces and watch them walk around the rest of the day feeling like royalty. NOTHING will ever beat that feeling for me. Make your goals, your wishes and wants. Make a plan to get there and go for it. When you achieve them the feeling is amazing and you will never forget it!

Printed in the United States
By Bookmasters